INDIANS of the ROCKY MOUNTAIN PARKS

INDIANS of the ROCKY MOUNTAIN PARKS

HUGH A. DEMPSEY

FIFTH
HOUSE
PUBLISHERS

Front cover image courtesy Glenbow Archives / NA-7-124
Back cover image courtesy Glenbow Archives / NA-1902-1
Cover and interior design by Brian Smith / Articulate Eye

The publisher gratefully acknowledges the support of the Department of Canadian Heritage and The Canada Council for the Arts for our publishing program.

We acknowledge the financial support of the Government of Canada through the Book Publishing Industry Development Program for our publishing activities.

Printed in Canada.

98 99 00 01 02 / 5 4 3 2 1

CANADIAN CATALOGUING IN PUBLICATION DATA

Dempsey, Hugh, A., 1929–

Indians of the Rocky Mountain parks

Includes bibliographical references.

ISBN 1-894004-10-8

1. Indians of North America–Rocky Mountains, Canadian (B.C. and Alta.)* 2. Indians of North America–Rocky Mountains, Canadian (B.C. and Alta.)–Pictorial works.* I. Title.

E78.R63D45 1998   971.1'00497   C98-910354-4

FIFTH
HOUSE
PUBLISHERS

Fifth House Ltd.
#9 - 6125 11th St. SE
Calgary, AB, Canada
    T2H 2L6
    1-800-360-8826

Table of Contents

Acknowledgements

five years, Pauline. She has been my patient supporter, my critic, my proofreader, and my salvation whenever something needed to be translated from Blackfoot to English, or some aspect of her culture explained.

My thanks also go to friends of an earlier era who helped me in my search for historical knowledge; Kootenay tribe; my father-in-law James Gladstone and other members of the Blood Tribe; One Gun, Ben Calf Robe, and Ayoungman from the Blackfoot; John Yellowhorn and Pat Bad Eagle from the Peigans; and George Maclean from the Stoneys. They were the real historians of their tribes.

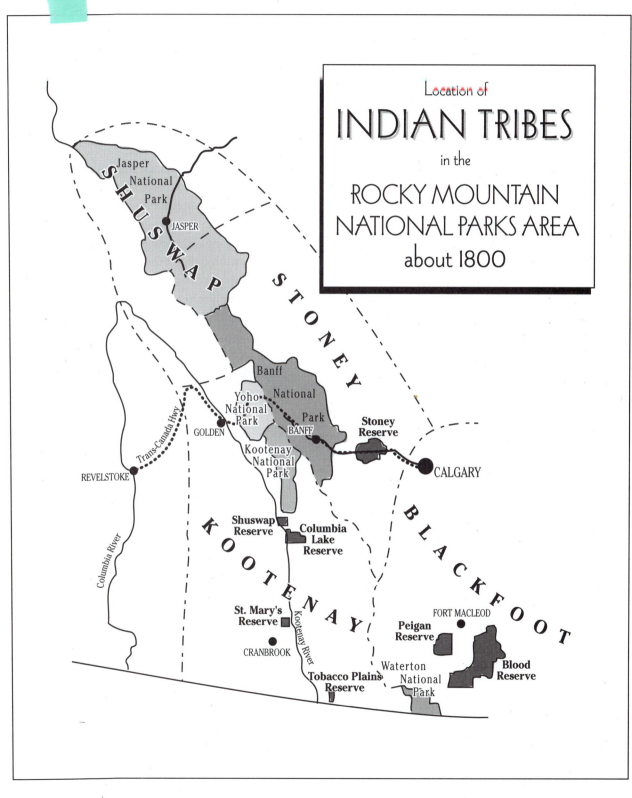

Location of

INDIAN TRIBES

in the

ROCKY MOUNTAIN NATIONAL PARKS AREA

about 1800

What's In a Name?

Within the past two decades, many Native groups have expressed dissatisfaction with tribal names and titles used by government officials, anthropologists, and the general public. For generations, these terms were in common use, as was the word "Indian" even though Columbus was lost when he introduced it. Today, some Native leaders and administrators are using tribal names developed from their own language. Hence, the Stoneys are the Nakoda First Nation, Kootenays the Ktunaxa First Nation, and Shuswap the Secwepemc First Nation, while the Blackfoot Nation is the Saukuitapix, or Prairie People. The latter group is divided into three tribes—the Blackfoot proper or Siksika First Nation, Bloods or Kainaiwa First Nation, and Peigan or Peigan First Nation.

Other terms such as "Native," "Aboriginal," "Indigenous," and "Native American" have all found varying degrees of acceptance and popularity in Native communities. As time passes, some may become universally accepted but the process of self-identification is still ongoing, and even better terms than the ones now in use may yet come into play. To avoid confusion, this book uses the terms and expressions that have come down through historical records and writings, not only by Europeans, but by Native peoples themselves. We hope readers will accept the use of these terms with their traditional meanings.

Introduction

A Stoney hunter gazing at the rugged peaks of the Rocky Mountains, or a Blackfoot war party travelling through a narrow mountain pass may seem to conjure overly romantic images of Indians, yet they truly reflect a part of the history of the Canadian Rockies. Before European explorers and fur traders arrived in the West, the areas now encompassed by Jasper, Banff, Waterton, Yoho, and Kootenay National Parks were the hunting grounds of four major tribes: the Kootenays, Shuswaps, Stoneys, and Blackfoot. The Kootenays made their home west of the Great Divide and south of Lake Windermere, while the Shuswaps occupied lands immediately to the north. The Stoneys, or Assiniboine Indians, resided on the east side of the Rockies in an area that extended from Jasper Park to the south end of Banff Park, and beyond. The tribes of the Blackfoot nation—primarily the Peigans and Bloods—lived to the south of the Stoney lands. In addition, Snare Indians, Woodland Crees, Métis, and Iroquois hunters occupied the region at various times.

These four tribes were often at war with each other. Sometimes they made short-lived peace treaties, but usually they were kept busy guarding their hunting grounds and making periodic incursions into enemy territory. The Kootenays, in particular, made regular visits to the Alberta and Montana prairies to hunt buffalo. Sometimes they did so under a pact of peace with the Blackfoot, while at other times they took their chances. In fact, the Waterton River is known to the Blackfoot as "Where We Fought the Kootenays," which confirms the hunting expeditions weren't always peaceful.

The Kootenays and Shuswaps lived in the same general region of the mountains and had much in common in the way they hunted, fished, and travelled. The main difference was that the Shuswaps tended to remain in their own hunting grounds and seldom went to war, but the same could not always be said for the Kootenays. On the other side of the mountains, the hunting areas of the Stoneys varied; some bands, like the Goodstoneys, were primarily foothills and mountain hunters, much like the Kootenays, while others, like the Bearspaw band, preferred the open plains, where they could live off the buffalo. In contrast, the Blackfoot were almost entirely plains dwellers. They retreated to the foothills for the winter months and ventured into the mountains only when they needed tepee poles, earth paints, or the valuable skins of bighorn sheep and mountain goats. The foothills and mountain dwellers often came into conflict with the Kootenays, while the plainsmen fought the Blackfoot and their allies on a regular basis.

The languages of all four groups are as different as French is to Chinese, or English to Arabic. The Kootenays speak their own dialect, unrelated to any other Indian dialect in the region. The Shuswaps are part of a linguistic group known as the Athapaskans, which includes their neighbours to the west—the Lilloets, Thompsons, Okanagans, and Lake Indians. Anthropologists refer to these five tribes collectively as the Interior Salish. The Stoneys speak a dialect of the Sioux language and at one time in the distant

George Maclean, or Walking Buffalo, is seen on the Stoney Reserve, looking out over the Bow River valley in 1910. He

Indians from his reserve, constantly working to gain better conditions for his people. He became chief of the Bearspaw band, acted as interpreter for the Indian agency, and participated in religious and social events.

—*Provincial Archives of Alberta, P.62.*

British artist Sydney P. Hall sketched a band of Blackfoot Indians fording the Bow River at Blackfoot Crossing in 1881. This engraving, made from the sketch, conforms closely to Hall's work. At the time of making the sketch, Hall was accompanying the governor general, the Marquis of Lorne, on a tour of the West.

—*Glenbow Archives, NA-1190-9.*

past were a part of that great nation. The Blackfoot are of Algonkian linguistic stock and their language is completely different again from those of the Kootenays, Shuswaps, and Stoneys. The tribes used sign language to communicate with each other, although some of the interior tribes also learned the Chinook jargon, a trading language developed by the coastal Indians.

Of central importance to these tribes were the Rocky Mountains, spectacular to view but often a desperate place to live. In winter, snows blocked the mountain passes and storms raged down from the snowy peaks. Bears and marmots, important food sources, went into hibernation in the late autumn and even the lowly rabbit seemed to disappear from the scene for the long winter months. An Indian, or

PLACE NAMES WITH A NATIVE ORIGIN

Many familiar place names in the national parks reflect a strong Native presence in the area.

National Park	Place Name	Indian Meaning
Waterton	Akamina Pass	High Bench Land
Banff	Mt. Assiniboine	Named for the Stoney Tribe
	Lake Minnewanka	Lake of the Spirits
	Minewakum Lake	Cascade Lake
	Mistaya River	Bear River
	Skoki Valley	Marsh Valley
	Sun Dance Creek	Sun Dance Creek
Jasper	Snaring River	Named for the Snare Indians
	Poboktan Mountain	Owl Mountain
	Sunwapta Falls	Turbulent River
Yoho	Amiskwi River	Beaver River
	Kiwetinok River	North Side River
	Waputik Ice Fields	Mountain Goat Ice Fields
	Wapta Lake	River Lake
Kootenay	Kootenay River	Named for the Kootenay Indians
	Misko Creek	Red Creek
	Tokumm Creek	Red Fox Creek

anyone else, would have been hard pressed to live in the high mountains all year round. In fact, in winter the Kootenays and Shuswaps usually retreated to the much friendlier valleys of the Kootenay and Columbia rivers; on the other side of the mountains, the Stoneys and Blackfoot wintered in the foothills. By late spring, with snows melting and icy waters tumbling down the mountainsides, the mountain tribes once again ventured into the high country to seek bighorn sheep, mountain goats, marmots, and other creatures that provided food and sustenance.

Pit house excavations indicate that some Indians, probably Shuswaps, wintered as far into the mountains as Banff town site, and fur traders record that other Shuswaps lived in the wide valleys of the Yellowhead Pass. Tall stumps of trees found at a few historic campsites indicate the snows were deep when the Indians wintered there. Sometimes the stumps are two metres high, showing the excessive snowfalls that must have confronted families, possibly trapped in the mountains by early snows.

The first Europeans these Indians met were fur traders and explorers. The existence of Athabasca and Yellowhead passes made the Jasper and Windermere areas main traffic routes to the Pacific for the Europeans and brought them into close contact with the Native inhabitants. They eventually became trading partners. The trading posts of Jasper House and Rocky Mountain House served the tribes on the east side of the Rockies, while Kootenae House was the trading centre for the western tribes. In the 1860s, gold miners invaded the mountains and brought more change to the lives of the Indians, but the biggest change occurred in the early 1880s when the Canadian Pacific Railway was constructed. With the destruction of the buffalo herds and the depletion of big game hunting, the Indians were obliged to settle on reserves in various parts of Alberta and British Columbia.

There, some learned to farm and ranch, while many continued to trap and fish. Government reports for 1912 record the changes in their lives. For the Kootenays: "Farming and stock-raising are the principal industries. Many hunt and trap, and others find work in the lumber camps and receive good wages." For the Shuswaps: "They follow farming and stock-raising; they also freight for the merchants and work on the neighbouring farms for the settlers, and a few hunt and trap." For the Stoneys: "These Indians raise cattle and horses, cut fire-wood and rails, which they deliver on car at Morley and Ozada stations. When saw-mills are running they also deliver logs to them. A number of Stonies are employed the year round at Kananaskis and Exshaw in connection with the lime kilns and cement works, and the ranchers along the foothills employ a number during haying season. The Indians were away for two months last fall on the annual hunt." For the Blackfoot tribes: "The occupations are cattle-raising, farming, hay-making, freighting, working for farmers adjoining the reserve, and beet-pulling."[1]

Children began attending residential schools in the late nineteenth century, and by the mid-twentieth century many were attending colleges and universities and receiving a professional education. Others continued to farm, ranch, and utilize the natural resources in their communities. Today, most participate in pow-wows, Indian Days, and other gatherings that reinforce their cultural heritage. They have a proud history and have contributed significantly to the regions now occupied by Canada's national parks in the Rocky Mountains.

The Nakoda, or Stoney Indians

The Stoney Indians have been associated with Banff ever since they put on their first show for tourists in 1889. This performance grew into the world famous Banff Indian Days, which were a part of Banff life until well into the twentieth century. Each year thousands of people came to admire the Indians on parade, photographing them in their colourful costumes, strolling through their tepee village, and watching them compete in horse racing, foot racing, archery, and other activities.

The Stoneys are part of the Sioux nation which has three branches—the *Dakota*, the *Lakota*, and the *Nakoda*. The Stoneys are Nakoda, also called the Yanktonnais. Their name is derived from the term *Assinipwat*, meaning "Stone People." This term also is the source of their other name, the Assiniboine. They separated from their parent tribe near the Great Lakes in the 1600s and became allies of the Cree nation. By the early 1700s, they had migrated west to the Rocky Mountains where they found excellent hunting and trapping along the foothills. Another group was said to have travelled across the plains of the Dakotas and Montana and ultimately became the Chiniki and Bearspaw bands.

By the mid-1800s, the Stoneys were divided into a number of small bands, usually named after their leaders. To the south, near Banff National Park, lived the Bearspaw, Chiniki, and Goodstoney bands; to the north lived the Sharphead band; and east of Jasper National Park lived the bands of Paul and Alexis, who spent their entire time in the foothills and woods, seldom venturing onto the plains.

In defence of their lands or when raiding enemy horse herds, the Stoneys often fought the Kootenays, Blackfoot, and Shuswaps. In 1901, a visitor remarked: "The Stonies, like all hill tribes, are independent and unconquerable, fierce fighters and mighty hunters, possessing great physical courage and stoical endurance, qualities which all men admire, and which characterize all great peoples. They are true highlanders winning courage from the perils of the fords and precipices, difficult trails and strenuous weather of the mountains, where roam the big game by which they live."[2]

Most of their stories of adventure related to warfare or hunting. For example, Joseph Jonas told of three Stoney men who trapped a war party of Bloods stealing their horses. The Stoneys had only one flintlock gun among them, but the Bloods did not know that. It was raining at the time, and when the first Stoney tried to load the gun, it exploded and killed him. A second Stoney picked up the weapon and started to shoot at the Bloods. In the meantime, the Bloods found they could not shoot back, as their powder was wet. The Stoneys, on the other hand, kept their powder dry and shot twenty of their enemy before the rest of them finally escaped.[3]

A hunting story was also told by Walking Buffalo. In the mid-1800s, two Stoneys named Hector Crawler and Crow's Breast were hunting in what is now the Banff town site, just where the railway crosses the Bow River, when they saw a grizzly bear on the other side of the stream. They decided to have some fun with the animal so they waded to the middle of the river where the beast came after them. As they were floating downstream, they got on each side of the bear, and every time it lunged at one man, the other grabbed it and turned it around in the water. They floated in this fashion for about half a mile, but when they came to shallow water they could no longer control the bear, so Crawler stabbed it with his knife. Then they dragged the carcass to shore where they skinned it and took the meat.[4]

The average Stoney tepee was smaller and lower than those of the nearby Blackfoot tribes. It was designed to hold a single family group and was often made of moose hide. However, the Bearspaw—the Plains branch of the family—preferred lodges made of buffalo hides. The tepee was owned by the woman of the household and it was her responsibility to put it up and take it down. It consisted of ten to sixteen poles, and was made by binding three poles as a tripod and leaning the other poles against it. Two more poles were used to control the air vents, or ears, at the top of the tepee; these poles slipped into tiny pockets sewn into the ears. In this way, the ears could be shifted to control the draft and the smoke.

Because they usually dwelt in the wooded foothills or mountains, the Stoneys made extensive use of fur-bearing animals. Beaver and mountain-sheep skins were made into robes, and otter pelts made good head coverings. Historian John Laurie described the clothing of the Stoneys in the 1840s:

> The men wore breechcloths or aprons about their middle, sometimes both garments, sometimes one or the other. Leggings, resembling the 'chaps' of the cowboy, covered their legs and were fastened by thongs to a belt. Some men wore skin shirts and most used a fur robe in winter. The women wore a long dress of tanned skins, bound at the waist by a belt, and moccasins whose high tops reached almost to the knee. Often they made an effort to ornament their garments with trade beads, shells, elk or beaver teeth.[5]

Besides buffalo, the Stoneys hunted moose, deer, elk, bear, mountain goat, bighorn sheep, and mountain lion for their meat requirements. They also trapped porcupines, rabbits, marmots, and small game animals, and fished the many lakes and streams that dotted their hunting grounds. The kidneys were also used as food, and often eaten raw. Boiled moose nose soup, roasted buffalo tongues, and cooked beaver tails were special delicacies.

Stoneys in the Jasper Park and Kootenay Plains area used fish traps at spawning time to catch trout, jackfish, and suckers. A barricade of sticks and brush was placed across a stream at an angle, forcing the fish into a slightly raised pond. From there, the fish had to jump into the next pond, but, while they were still in the air, the fishermen caught them in their hands and tossed them onto the bank. There they were filleted, dried, and stored for winter use.

Among the fruits and vegetables the Stoneys favoured were all kinds of berries, including saskatoons, cranberries, and chokecherries. These were eaten fresh, dried into patties, stewed, or dried and mixed with dried buffalo meat and fat to make pemmican. Mushrooms, bullrush roots, tiger lily bulbs, wild carrots, and wild onions were also roasted and eaten.

Of all the tribes in the Alberta plains and foothills, the Stoneys were the first to be converted to Christianity. They were visited by Methodist missionary Robert Rundle in 1841 and two of their most prominent leaders, Tchakta and Two Young Men, became converts. Several years later, when the Earl of Southesk was hunting along the foothills, he was surprised to hear some Stoney Indians singing hymns. "They are Christians," he observed, "having had some teaching from Protestant missionaries, and seem to be most religious, excellent people."[6]

Southesk noted that in the evening, a bell was rung in the Stoney camp and a church service was held by the Indians in their own language, after which more hymns were sung.

The first permanent Stoney mission was established in 1079 at Morley, just east of Banff National Park. The Bearspaw, Chiniki, and Goodstoney bands signed Treaty No. Seven with the Canadian government in 1877 and then took a reserve in the Morley area. Farther north, Alexis, Paul, and Sharphead signed their names to Treaty No. Six a year later. They, in turn, took reserves near Lake Wabamun, Lac Ste. Anne, and Wolf Creek.

The Bearspaw, Chiniki, and Goodstoney bands were issued with tools in the hope that they would become farmers, but their reserve was close to the mountains, where the temperatures were too cool for crops to ripen. Besides, most of the Stoneys preferred to hunt in the mountains, foothills, and plains as long as there was big game to be found. The Goodstoney band preferred the Kootenay Plains for their hunting grounds and in 1892 one of its leaders, Peter Wesley, abandoned his reserve and took his followers to live permanently on the plains. Finally, in 1947, they were given the Bighorn Reserve west of Rocky Mountain House. Similarly, a number of Bearspaw's followers preferred to hunt on the upper waters of the Highwood River and they eventually were given the Eden Valley Reserve in the 1940s.

Even though the Stoneys may have been isolated from European settlement during the early years, this changed in 1883 when the Canadian Pacific Railway was built through the middle of their reserve, to be followed many years later by the Trans-Canada Highway. As a result of improved access, visitors often dropped by to see the progress of the tribe. In 1895, for example, a reporter examined life on the Stoney Reserve, visiting the Indian agent's office, the slaughter house where rations were issued, the residential school, and individual homes. "Each adult is allowed a pound [of beef] a day and the children a proportionate amount," he said when he witnessed the Stoneys being rationed. "The cattle are shot at the slaughter house and hung up for half an hour to bleed, then skinned and cut up. The bulk of the cattle are supplied by Mr. D. McDougall, who has had the contract for some time past, but the Stonies have upwards of 700 head of their own, and a considerable number of these are used for beef."[7]

The reporter was then taken on a tour of the reserve. "One of the most interesting features of the visit was a drive through the Indian villages, of which there are three, under the respective chieftainship of Bear's Paw, Chiniquay, and Jonas. The houses are neat, one storey log buildings, the logs squared and painted white, and the roofs generally shingled."[8]

Another contact with the outside world occurred in 1889, when a washout on the CPR line stranded a large number of tourists at Banff. According to a story told by Tom Wilson, arrangements were made for 250 Stoneys to come to the Banff Springs Hotel to entertain the bored tourists. The Indians camped along the Bow River below Bow Falls and remained there for about a week, offering horse races, foot races, tugs-of-war, parades, and dancing. So successful was the show that the Stoneys were invited to return for the 24th of May and Dominion Day celebrations. "By 1902," said historian Jon Whyte, "whole families were arriving, and some 200 Stoneys made an encampment at their traditional camp site near Minnehappa, the waterfall on Cascade Mountain."[9]

About 1908 the Banff Indian Days became an annual event, held in July immediately after the Calgary Stampede. Over the years, many events were added to the celebration, such as dancing competitions, rodeo, concerts, and pageants. The Banff Springs Hotel built a grandstand near the athletic grounds where guests could watch the dancers, singers, and cultural demonstrations. Some of the prominent names associated with the Indian Days were Hector Crawler, Walking Buffalo, John Hunter, Hanson Bearspaw, and Joshua and William Twin. In 1922, when Governor General Lord Byng visited the Indian Days, a reporter described the scene:

Upwards of 600 Indians were in line in the

clothed in all the barbaric splendor the resources of the tribe could command. Many of the chiefs and councillors were garbed in almost priceless costumes of buckskin, tanned to a softness of silk, beadwork and feather headdresses, while some of the braves were attired only in war paint and breech clouts. Here and there in the procession might be seen a woman leading a pony hitched to a travois on which were one or more children.[10]

The Banff Indian Days ended in 1978, to be replaced by the Stoneys' own pow-wows and celebrations on their own reserve. Even so, these Indians have remained inextricably linked with Banff National Park, just as they have been an integral part of the environment for the past three hundred years.

Today, the Stoneys have prospered from natural gas discoveries on their land and from

have also suffered from living on the main line of the Trans-Canada Highway, their reserve sliced by two major highways, a rail line, and power lines. A traditional and friendly people, they try to keep to themselves but willingly participate in any cultural or tourist programs to which they are invited. They have their own village at the annual Calgary Stampede and conduct several pow-wows and rodeos a year, in their modern arenas.

STONEY LEGENDS OF THE BANFF AREA

The ghostly sounds of singing, drumming, and hoofbeats have contributed to Stoney legends of the Banff area. For example, Indians visiting the Banff Hot Springs sometimes heard singing, or the sounds of an eagle bone whistle of the type used at the Sun Dance. "We would wait around, trying to see who it was and what was making the sounds," recalled Stoney patriarch Walking Buffalo, "but we could never see anything in the waters."[11]

The Stoneys bathed in the warm waters of the spring or gathered yellow ochre nearby to use as face paint. Before they left, they dropped offerings into the water to thank the spirits for the use of the hot springs and the paint.

Devil's Head Mountain, at Lake Minnewanka, is considered sacred because its sides are always bare of snow, even in the middle of winter. The lake, whose name means "Lake of the Spirits," was a place where the Stoneys could hear voices but no one was ever seen. According to Enoch Baptiste, "One time when our people were camping near the lake, my father heard what seemed to be the beating of a drum. The noise seemed to be coming from the water. He could also hear voices down in the lake … Soon my father saw, near the centre of the lake, a strange creature rise out of the water. It was half fish and half human being. As my father stood watching, the fish-person sank back into the lake."[12]

At Ghost River, just east of the park, a camp of Stoneys heard the sounds of buffalo, as though they were being herded past the camp. Each night the sound was repeated, but when people went outside their tepees, nothing could be seen. One evening a hunter promised to find the source of the strange sounds. He saddled his horse and tied it next to his lodge. As soon as he heard the sounds of hoofbeats, he jumped on his horse and pursued the herd. Ahead he saw the buffalo and a man riding a grey horse. He spurred his own horse forward, trying to get a glimpse of the stranger's face, but as soon as he caught up with him, the man and the buffalo disappeared. Ever since that incident, the nearby stream has been called Ghost River.

This spectacular view shows a Stoney encampment near Mount Wilson, on the North Saskatchewan River, about 1920. The women were responsible for the tepees and pack horses while the men were away hunting.

—*Whyte Museum of the Canadian Rockies, 263/NA71-5985.*

Amos Bigstoney and family were photographed at the base of Cascade Mountain, Banff, in 1889. The Stoney boy at right holds a knife scabbard which is decorated with brass studs.

—*Glenbow Archives, NA-637-3.*

James Bigstoney, left, and Paul Rider, posed for photographer A.B. Thom in the 1890s. Bigstoney has painted both his face and his horse and wears a shirt decorated with hawk feathers. Hanging from Rider's wrist is a whip made of leather and wood, and decorated with brass studs.

—*Glenbow Archives, NA-2084-59.*

INDIAN TEEPEES,
MORLEY,
ALTA.

W. KILROE,
PHOTO.
Calgary.

Louisa Hunter and daughters pose in front of their tepee at the west end of the Stoney Reserve, about 1910. All three are dressed in their everyday clothes, which feature cotton dresses and wide leather belts with brass studs. These studs were used as decoration as they were durable, inexpensive, and obtainable from any harness maker's shop.

—H. Dempsey Collection.

Stoney women enjoy the sports events at the Banff Indian Days in the 1920s. The kerchiefs and blankets or shawls were part of both the ceremonial and everyday wear of the women.

—United Church of Canada Archives, 93.049 P/781N.

This Stoney girl has adapted a number of Stoney items for her costume at the Banff Indian Days in the 1920s. She wears a woollen dress with a yoke festooned with tubular glass beads, elk teeth, and brass bells. To this she has added, around her waist, a basket-weave cape that is usually worn over the shoulders, and, on her head, a porcupine hair headdress that was worn by male dancers. Such adaptation of cultural objects during parades and competitions was not unusual.

—*Glenbow Archives, NA-714-142.*

Peter Wesley was a Stoney chief who rebelled against the dictates of the Indian agent and in 1892 he took a number of his followers northward into the wilderness of the Kootenay Plains. Over the next several decades they refused to return, until at last in 1947 they were given their own Bighorn Reserve in their traditional hunting grounds. Note that Wesley is wearing the military-type uniform issued to chiefs.

—United Church of Canada Archives, 93.049 P/777.

A Stoney family on the trail prepares a meal in front of their small hunting tepee, about 1910. Each has dressed in their best finery for the photographer. The woman's yoke is fully beaded while the boy wears a buckskin outfit with beaded strips and leggings. The child at left wears a woollen dress with a beaded yoke. The man of the lodge hasn't dressed for the occasion; he simply added an animal skin bandolier to his cotton shirt and donned his fringed leggings.

—United Church of Canada Archives, 93.049 P/782N.

John Hunter (in beaded vest), George Maclean, and family prepare a meal on the Stoney Reserve in 1927. Note that the children's clothing resembles those of adults. The two girls at left wear shawls while the boy has a traditional Hudson's Bay blanket coat. The older girl has the responsibility of caring for the baby and carries him in a fold of the shawl, held in place by a leather strap.

—*H. Dempsey Collection.*

While they were hunting, the Stoneys seldom stayed in one place very long, which meant that everything they owned had to be moved easily. Fresh meat would soon spoil, so it was sun-dried on racks for later use. Here, Sarah Twoyoungmen demonstrates the method of drying meat at the Banff Indian Days in 1942.

—*Glenbow Archives, NA-1241-739.*

This is a view of a Stoney encampment at Banff Indian Days shortly after the turn of the century. Note that most of the tepees are unpainted. Only later did the organizers of the event give special prizes to those who painted their lodges.

—*Glenbow Archives, NA-4891-1.*

This decorative pictograph on the side of John Hunter's tepee depicts the various activities which take place in a Stoney camp. The family is cooking, hunting, singing, and drumming—all under a symbol of the sun.

—*Glenbow Archives, NA-7-149.*

The Stoney Indians had colourful designs for tepees which they took to the Banff Indian Days and the Calgary Stampede. This 1910 camp at Banff shows one feature which distinguishes the tepees from those of the Blackfoot, their traditional enemies. Stoney tepees have pockets in the ears to control the smoke hole at the top, while the Blackfoot tepees have an eyelet that enables the pole to project through it. This knowledge could be vital in times of war, for if a person stumbled upon a strange camp, he could immediately tell if they were friend or foe.

—*Provincial Archives of Alberta, P.38.*

Stoneys prepare to move camp from Indian Flats, just south of Canmore, in the 1890s. Using only pack horses to carry their gear, they will leave the tepee poles standing for the use of the next hunting party that comes along.

—United Church of Canada Archives, 93.049 P/761N.

This Stoney hunting party was far from their reserve when they were photographed at Pincher Creek in 1895. The tribe hunted all along the east slopes of the Rockies, from the United States border to Jasper National Park. The hunting party included men, women, children, extra horses, and dogs. The party stayed away from their reserve all summer, living off deer, elk, mountain goats, and mountain sheep while they travelled from one hunting area to another.

—Glenbow Archives, NA-1129-5.

This Stoney has the typical gear of an Indian hunter in the 1890s. He carries a repeating rifle, skinning knife, and revolver, wears a Hudson's Bay blanket coat, and carries a braided horse hair halter.

—Glenbow Archives, NA-2084-61.

John Hunter was a leading chief of the Stoney tribe. Besides being a rancher, he was a noted hunter and is seen here with everything he needed for a mountain hunt.

—*H. Dempsey Collection.*

Stoney hunters display their trophies of bighorn sheep in the Kootenay Plains in 1904. Left to right are Silas Abraham, Moses Wesley, and Sampson Beaver. Although they hunted for food, they also acted as guides to white hunters who were seeking trophy heads.

—Glenbow Archives, NA-1263-9.

Mark Poucette, of the Stoney tribe, poses with a hunting bow and arrows. He wears a horned headdress and a necklace made of brass and tile beads.

—*Glenbow Archives, NA-1296-5.*

Joseph Twoyoungmen was a respected elder and ceremonialist of the Stoney tribe when this photograph
was taken in the 1920s. He carries a pipe-axe made of
catlinite stone, a copy of brass ones sold by traders.
The pipe-axe symbolized a choice facing the owner,
the pipe representing peace and the axe signifying
war. Twoyoungmen, however, used his pipe only for
ceremonial pipe smoking purposes.

—*United Church of Canada Archives, 93.049 P/778.*

These Stoney Indians travelled for several
days by wagon in 1922 to attend a fair in
the Windermere Valley with their onetime
enemies, the Kootenays. The horse travois,
easily assembled for a parade, was later
taken apart and the poles used for their
tepee.

—*Glenbow Archives, NA-1135-17.*

John Hunter, or Sitting Eagle, was a successful Stoney rancher who enjoyed participating in the Banff Indian Days and the Calgary Stampede. He is seen here at the Stampede in the 1920s. A handsome man, he was one of the most photographed Indians on the Stoney Reserve, and was the subject of many paintings and sculptures.

—Glenbow Archives, Lupson Collection, NA-667-917A.

Stoney Indians race horses bareback at Morley in front of the impressive range of the Rocky Mountains. This view was taken in 1910 by Elliot Barnes.

—*Whyte Museum of the Canadian Rockies, 48/NA66-1581.*

A young Stoney Indian poses against the beautiful backdrop of the Rocky Mountains at the Banff Indian Days in 1924.

—Glenbow Archives, Dan McCowan Collection, NA-7-124.

George Maclean, or Walking Buffalo, was educated at the Stoney residential school and named for Methodist missionary John Maclean. Well educated and fluent in English and Stoney, he was one of the most popular figures at the Banff Indian Days. He was so conversant with cameras that on one occasion when an amateur photographer was having trouble, he took the camera, made the necessary adjustments, and handed it back. He then resumed his pose as a stoic Indian.

—Glenbow Archives, NA-667-893.

Stoneys gather beside the Banff Springs Hotel for their performances in 1941. The Banff Indian Days was a featured attraction at the park for more than seventy years.

—Glenbow Archives, Gully Collection, NA-1241-642.

The Stoney Indians, seen here at the Banff Springs Hotel in 1941, were proud of the white buckskin clothing and exquisite beadwork. Each year, until the Banff Indian Days ended in 1976, they vied for honours awarded for costumes, dances, and races. Walking Buffalo, a Stoney patriarch and head chief, is seen standing at right.

—Glenbow Archives, Gully Collection, NA-1241-754.

The Ktunaxa, or Kootenay Indians

The Kootenays, or *Ktunaxa*, of the Rocky Mountains are part of a large nation that extends south and west into Montana and Idaho. Those living closest to the Rockies were known as the Upper Kootenays or *Skalsi'ulk* people. They drew much of their lifestyle and culture from the Great Plains on the east side of the mountains. They relied, in part, upon the buffalo for food and used horses, conical skin lodges, buckskin clothing, feather headdresses, the Sun Dance, and other traditions associated with the Plains peoples. In contrast, their fellow tribesmen, the Lower Kootenays, used grass lodges, birch bark canoes, and clothing woven from rushes. The dividing line between the two groups was drawn through Kootenai Falls in northwestern Montana.

The *Skalsi'ulk* were divided into a number of smaller bands, usually named after the territory they occupied. The Columbia Lake, St. Mary's River, Tobacco Plains, and Michel Prairie bands lived in Canada. Their winter campsites were located on the Kootenay and Columbia rivers, but in summer they ranged far into the Rockies and out onto the Alberta plains near Waterton and Banff National Parks.

Just east of Banff National Park is an area known as the Kootenay Plains where Kootenay Indians brought their furs to barter with the North West Company before trading posts were built on the west side of the Rockies. Even earlier, the site was probably used for intertribal trading, for there are traditions among the Kootenays of meetings with Crees to exchange tobacco and other goods. In 1811, in the same general area along the Clearwater River,

fur trader Alexander Henry noticed "the remains of some of the dwellings of the Kootenays, built of wood, straw, and pine branches. The same are observed along Rivière de la jolie Prairie and Ram River. This gives us every reason to suppose that nation formerly dwelt along the foot of these mountains, and even as far down as our present establishment [Rocky Mountain House], near which the remains of some of their lodges are still to be seen."[13] Explorer John Palliser saw the same kind of temporary lodges in 1858 after crossing the summit of the Rockies above Kananaskis Lakes.

Of the four Kootenay bands, the Michel Prairie band, which became extinct in the mid-1700s, was known to have resided permanently on the prairie side of the mountains. Also called the *Tunáxa*, they occupied the area from Crowsnest Pass to Waterton National Park and extended their hunting as far north as where Calgary is now located, and as far east as Lethbridge. Horses had not yet arrived from the Spanish settlements in Mexico, so the Michel Prairie people travelled on foot, used snowshoes in winter, and raised dogs for pack animals. In the summer, they travelled through the mountain passes to fish and hunt for big game in the Columbia Lakes region. Regretfully, they were struck down by a smallpox epidemic about 1730 and the band was virtually exterminated.

The first white man to record visiting a Kootenay camp was explorer Peter Fidler. In 1792, he travelled with a party of Peigans to meet some Kootenays who wanted to exchange horses for European trade goods. Their camp, consisting of seven lodges, was located on the east side of the Rocky Mountains, just north of the Crowsnest Pass. Fidler noted that the Kootenay tepees were the same as those used by Plains Indians, only smaller. He also noted a few facts about their way of life:

The Cottonahew makes their dishes or roggans of the inner bark of the Pine, some of them are made of Pine roots, others of Grass, made in a very neat manner & water tight. They have several curious shapes of these culinary utensils, some being made exactly in the form of a Tea Kettle wanting the neck. In these they boil their provisions, meat, by immersing hot stones into it & boiling it in that manner.

The Implements they have for getting wood consists of a Red Deers [elk] horn all the branches being broke off except the long one next the Head. This is sharpened like a chissel by rubbing it upon stones & this constitutes their hatchet. They have also wedges made of the same materials with a stone fixed in a withey as a handle; with these they will very soon cut down a Tree & split or rive it into smaller pieces fit for firewood.

These people have a Tent for each wife, whom they visit occasionally. The reason they assign for this singular custom is that too many wives together never agree, which is good reasoning. This man had four. He was about 40 years of age, and of smaller stature. I was the first European they had ever seen.[14]

The Kootenays followed an annual cycle of activity, including salmon fishing, hunting, and berry picking. They hunted deer, elk, moose, bighorn sheep, and mountain goats in their own regions, and buffalo on the open plains to the east. They killed small game for food, collected the furs of beaver, otter, and other animals, and made use of all the natural resources their territory had to offer.

Although hunting on the west side of the Rockies was often a solitary activity, in the spring the Kootenays sometimes conducted communal deer hunts. For a successful hunt, a leader picked a narrow spot between two ridges and hunters erected a fence or barrier across the trail. Then hunters spread into a long line across the valley and drove the deer into the trap, where other hunters were waiting to make the kill. Afterwards, the slain animals were butchered and distributed evenly among the families. During the following days, the meat was prepared, dried, and stored away for future use. Another form of communal hunting occurred midsummer when hunters gathered in a grassy clearing and then sent two men with lighted torches to encircle the whole area with flames. Bowmen outside the circle of flames shot any deer that tried to escape, while others waited to kill the animals caught inside the fiery trap.

Elk were hunted in the late summer and early fall. After this hunt was finished, the Kootenays crossed the Rockies to hunt buffalo. If they were at war with the Peigans or Bloods, they sent scouts ahead to see if their enemies were nearby. When they were, the Kootenays sometimes tried to effect a temporary peace treaty, which was a risky undertaking. To accomplish this, a man carrying a pipe slipped through one of the mountain passes and furtively searched until he found an enemy camp. After sunset, he went to a nearby hill, erected a flag or banner, and sat with the pipe in his hands, waiting to be discovered the next morning. If he was unlucky, his enemies killed him on the spot. Often, however, wiser heads prevailed and he was invited to the chief's lodge, where a peace pact was made. The emissary then returned to his people with the gifts of tobacco he had received, and soon after the Kootenays rode out from the mountains, travelling in single file through one of the narrow passes. They pitched camp near their one-time enemies and a feast was held, at which time the Kootenays presented gifts of horses to their newfound friends. The two groups then separated, the Kootenays travelling out to the plains, sometimes as far as what now is Medicine Hat, to hunt buffalo, dry the meat, and carry it back across the mountains.

The Kootenays usually conducted two buffalo hunts a year, one in the spring and the other in the fall. If they were desperately short of food, they might also cross the mountains on snowshoes in winter to hunt in the Alberta foothills, but this was a dangerous practice because of the terrible condition of the mountain passes and the hostility of the Peigans. Farther north, the Kootenay crossed the mountains into what is now Banff National Park to hunt elk, deer, and moose. Here again, they had to be on the alert, for they were intruding upon the hunting grounds of the Stoney Indians.

When horses were introduced from Spanish settlements in the early 1700s, the Kootenays became excellent breeders and herders. Because their territory enjoyed a milder climate than the open plains, they were able to raise large numbers of the animals and became proficient horse traders. In 1858, John Palliser visited a small camp of eleven lodges near what now is Cranbrook, BC, and was surprised to discover they had a herd of five hundred horses. Palliser exchanged some of his travel-weary animals for Kootenay horses and only later discovered the ones he had obtained had been stolen in a recent raid against the Flathead Indians.

Because of their wealth in horses and their frequent trips into enemy territory, the Kootenays became accomplished warriors, both in their attacks and in the defence of their camps. There are numerous accounts of their battles with Stoneys, Bloods, Peigans, and other enemies, with the Kootenays often emerging victorious. For example, about 1820,

some Blackfoot and Kootenays met at the site of the present-day Prince of Wales Hotel in Waterton Park, to trade horses and other goods. When the Blackfoot began to pillage the Kootenays, the Kootenay leader, Not a Grizzly, shot and killed one of the Blackfoot. The Kootenays then retreated to their camp on the Waterton River where a pitched battle was fought; when it was over, thirty Blackfoot had been killed, but only four Kootenays were wounded.

The Kootenays are notable in their early acceptance of Christianity. In 1824, a Kootenay boy named Night Runner was taken to a mission school at the site of present-day Winnipeg and a few years later another boy, known only as Kootenay Collins, was also sent to that school. Then, in the year 1829–30, two Kootenays, Wolf Coming Up and Cow Buffalo Spirit, were said to have accompanied an American fur trading expedition to California, where they received religious instruction. By the time the first Christian missionaries arrived among them in the 1840s, the Kootenays were already observing Sunday as a holy day and performing their own interpretation of Christian prayers.

When explorer James Hector visited them in 1859, he noted, "They are all very religious, having been converted by the Roman Catholic priests. Frequently, and at stated times, a bell is rung in the camp, and all who are within hearing at once go down on their knees and pray."[15]

The Kootenay territory was invaded in the 1860s by gold miners who established camps on Wildhorse Creek. Reserves were allotted to the Kootenays, but so flagrant was their treatment at the hands of local settlers that in 1887 the North-West Mounted Police were sent to bring law and order to the community. They found many complaints of the chief, Isadore, to be justified, and exonerated a Kootenay wrongly charged with murder,

The Kootenays settled on four reserves: the

Columbia Lake Reserve, on Lake Windermere, and St. Mary's, Tobacco Plains, and Lower Kootenay reserves, all near Cranbrook. In 1887, the Indian agent stated that they had small farms, owned cattle and horses, and also lived by trapping, hunting, and working for local settlers. They continued to maintain their old practices as much as possible, but the introduction of residential schools, the depletion of fur-bearing animals, and the influx of farmers and settlers gradually forced a change in their way of life. Over the years, the tribe has been obliged to adopt more and more of the customs and activities of the white society around them. But they have been diligent in preserving the knowledge of their history and their pride in being members of the *Ktunaxa* nation.

THE WATER MONSTER

According to a Kootenay legend, in the days before there were people on earth, a huge water monster lived in Kootenay Lake. When it was hungry, it swam west to the Arrow Lakes, then north along the Columbia River and around to the area near Golden. It then continued south to Columbia Lake and followed the Kootenay River back to its home. Canal Flats did not exist in those days so the two rivers were all in one. Along the way the monster feasted on any creatures it could find in the water or on the land.

The havoc and destruction became so terrible that the creatures finally appealed to their Great Spirit, *Nalmu'qtse*, for help. He called them into a council and told them he would kill the water monster if they would help. When they descended upon the monster's lair, it fled up the Columbia to Boat Encampment, then turned back southward until it came to a small stream. Hoping to throw its pursuers off the track, the monster swam up to the headwaters of the brook. But *Nalmu'qtse* was not deceived and when he cornered the monster, he hurled a spear at it and struck it in the leg. The monster screamed in pain but pulled free and fled downstream, leaving the waters behind it running red with blood. Ever since then, the Kootenays have called this stream *Aiknosoka*, or Red Creek.

The monster dashed south to Lake Windermere where it suddenly turned up Morgeau Creek. As the creatures gathered at the mouth of the stream, *Nalmu'qtse* decided to send Coyote, the Cowardly One, to chase it out. Meanwhile, the monster had dug a deep hole at the headwaters of the creek, hoping to make a hiding place, but it struck solid rock and had to give up. That huge hole is still there today. Coyote tried to stop the water monster, but as soon as it roared, the Cowardly One fled and the dreaded creature swam back to the Columbia.

Nalmu'qtse realized they could chase the creature around and around from the Columbia to the Kootenay and back, so he went to the south end of Columbia Lake and scraped earth and rocks from the mountains at Findlay Creek to make a huge barrier, known today as Canal Flats. When the water monster swam south through Columbia Lake, it suddenly found it was trapped. Coyote, trying to redeem himself, approached the monster with his tomahawk, but when the creature roared, he dropped the weapon and fled. Quickly, Fox picked up the axe and delivered a crushing blow to the water monster's skull. Then all the other creatures swarmed over the body and tore it into a thousand pieces. Today, if one travels along the southeast shore of the lake, one can still see a large red spot under the water that marks the place where the monster was killed.

Nalmu'qtse then picked up a handful of dried blood and hurled it eastward towards the mountains, declaring that this would become a race of people with red skins. Wherever the pieces fell, they became a tribe of Indians. He then wiped his hands, and, as the flecks of blood dropped to the ground, he declared that these would become a great tribe of Indians known as the Kootenays. And so the Kootenay nation was born.[16]

Chief Isadore stands in front of his followers at Fort Steele in 1888. A year earlier, the Kootenays had been treated so badly by local settlers that the North-West Mounted Police had been sent to bring law and order to the community. They found many complaints of Chief Isadore were justified and exonerated a Kootenay wrongly charged with murder.

—Glenbow Archives, NA-1753-27.

Edward S. Curtis, famous western photographer, entitled this picture simply, "Kootenay Indian Girl." It was taken in 1910.

—Glenbow Archives, NA-1700-26.

This portrait of a Kootenay man was also taken by Edward S. Curtis in 1910.

Louis Capilo and his family are seen in camp, about 1917. They lived near the shores of Lake Windermere and left their cabin in favour of a tepee for the summer months. Note that these Kootenays are dressed in everyday clothes, without adornment, and even the baby is in a plain cradleboard.

—Glenbow Archives, NA-3078-22.

"Big Joe" David, seen here with his wife Mary Ann in the 1920s, was a conjuror in his younger years, treating the sick before becoming leader of the Sun Dance ceremonies. On one occasion he went to seek a vision, and while he slept, a spirit took him far downstream to the bottom of a waterfall and then to its top. When he awoke he followed the trail taken in his dream to seek spiritual power.

—*Glenbow Archives, NA-1897-4.*

Mary Madeline Isaacs, seen here, was a
granddaughter of Eneas Paul, or Big Knife,
leading chief of the Kootenays at Elmo,
Montana. She was a member of the
Tobacco Plains band. She wears a velvet
dress adorned with glass "bugle" beads,
tied with a woven l'Assomption sash
around her waist.

—*Glenbow Archives, NA-1902-1.*

This Kootenay mother, Cecile Gravelle, shows off her twin daughters, Elizabeth and Mary, both in the highly decorated cradle boards. The Kootenay were noted for the distinctiveness of their cradle boards and the quality of their beadworking.

—*Glenbow Archives, NA-1897-5.*

This Kootenay woman waits patiently for
the parade to begin at the Banff Indian
Days in the 1920s. The kerchief was a particular style of the mountain people.

—*Glenbow Archives, Dan McCowan Collection, NA-7-
35.*

These Kootenay men and women assembled in the Windermere valley for a celebration in 1922. Their costumes are an interesting mixture of Plateau and Plains Indian designs. Of all the mountain tribes, the Kootenays were the most closely associated with the buffalo hunting tribes to the east.

—*Glenbow Archives, NA-1135-9.*

Kootenay women line up with their horses at the David Thompson memorial celebration, held near Windermere in 1922. The richness and variety of their dresses and horse gear reflect their skill as bead and craft workers.

—*Glenbow Archives, NA-1135-10.*

These Kootenay women took part in celebrations at Windermere in 1922. Only one
has a beaded dress, but most wear the traditional head scarfs. Left to right, they are:
unknown, Ann Alpine, unknown, Mary
Madeline Arbell, Margaret Arbell, Mary
Jimmy, unknown, Catherine Sam, Suzette
Williams, and Sabina Alpine.

—*Glenbow Archives, NA-1135-11.*

Chief Louis Arbell gathers with Kootenay and Shuswap women for celebrations at Windermere in 1922. Those on horseback, left to right, are: unknown, Chief Arbell, Mrs. Cecile Bramall, Suzette Williams, Mrs. Christine Wight, unknown, Mrs. Christine Kinbasket, Metaline Jimmy, and Anna Pierre. The women standing in the front row are: Mrs. Sophie Williams, Mrs. Ethel Consaga, unknown, Helen Mission, Catherine Wight, and Lucy Michel. Note that Catherine Wight holds the same cradleboard that appears in another picture of Mrs. Ambroise Gravelle and her twins.

—Glenbow Archives, NA-1135-8.

David Paul, a leading chief of the Kootenays, is seen here in 1922. As a boy he attended a mission school at Couer d'Alene and when he graduated he became a strong supporter of the Catholic church. During his term as chief, he encouraged close cooperation with the priests and local settlers.

—*Glenbow Archives, NA-1135-14.*

Sophie Nicholas shows a strong Plains Indian emphasis in her costume and use of a horse travois. Only her head scarf and the short poles on her travois distinguish her from tribes in Alberta. This photograph was taken at Lake Windermere in 1922.

—Glenbow Archives, NA-1135-15.

Michael Michel proudly displays his dancing bustle and his beaded outfit decorated with uniquely Kootenay designs. Besides being an excellent dancer, Michel was remembered for his ability as a hunter and fisherman.

—Glenbow Archives, NA-1902-2.

These two Kootenay elders display their
finery at a dance in the 1920s. Even though
their outfits utilize Plains Indian objects,
such as eagle feather headdresses and
beaded leggings, their vests, gauntlets, and
moccasins bear uniquely Kootenay designs.

—*Glenbow Archives, NA-1135-46.*

**A hunting party of Kootenays cross the
CPR tracks at Donald, BC, about 1885. They
are dressed for the bitter winter weather
and one man has a pack of furs which he
has likely brought to trade.**

—*Glenbow Archives, NA-782-4.*

Little Jim, a Kootenay from Lake Windermere, exhibits a mountain lion he killed during a hunting expedition in 1919.

—*Glenbow Archives, NA-3078-23.*

The wife and child of Baptiste Mathias, Kootenay ceremonialist, are seen here in 1926. In later years, Baptiste Mathias had a dream instructing him to revive the Sun Dance but when he tried to bring the people together, there were not enough who knew the ceremony.

—*Glenbow Archives, NA-1897-8.*

This sweatlodge was used by Ambroise Gravelle, an elder of the Kootenay tribe, and was photographed near Flagstone, BC, in 1959. Gravelle was one of the leading historians of the Kootenays. He remembered seeing Native ceremonies being performed when he was a child in 1906, just before he was sent to St. Ignatius Residential School. He said the old ways never really died out in the face of Christianity.

On the open prairies near Lethbridge, Alberta, is this stone effigy marking the place where a prominent Kootenay chief was killed by Blood Indians. In 1862, the Bloods and Kootenays were at peace, but when a young Blood tried to steal a Kootenay horse, he was killed. His brother, a chief named Many Spotted Horses (seen in the 1855 sketch), vowed revenge, and when he met a Kootenay named White Horse, he shot and killed him. To commemorate the incident, the Bloods marked the place where the Kootenay fell.

—*H. Dempsey Collection.*

The Secwepemc, or Shuswap Indians

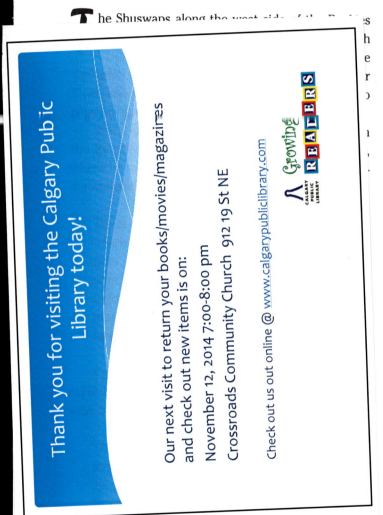

The Shuswaps along the west side of the Rockies

[...] Shuswap nation, who dwell near the Shushwap Lake and grand fork of the Thompson River in British Columbia. Separated from the main body of their tribe by 300 or 400 miles of almost impenetrable forest, they hold but little communication with them.[18]

These Shuswaps had moved into the Jasper Park area that once had been occupied by the Snare band. After that group was massacred by Stoney Indians in the 1840s [see sidebar], the *Texqokallt* extended their range across the Yellowhead Pass. However, they also suffered extensively from enemy attacks and disease, and by the time Doctor Cheadle met them, they had been reduced in number from thirty families to about thirty people. They were, he said, "peaceable and honest, ignorant of wickedness and war."[19] Ultimately, they too were exterminated and today they are listed as one of the extinct bands of the Shuswap nation.[20]

The Shuswaps lived by hunting bighorn sheep, mountain goats, elk, moose, deer, marmots, porcupines, and many small animals. One of their favourite game animals was the deer. It was hunted with bows and arrows and was butchered immediately after killing. The meat was then divided into nine pieces so that it could be carried easily. In winter, the deer pieces were wrapped in skin and dragged through the snow, while in summer, slits were cut in the meat so that it could be carried directly on a person's back. Back in camp, the meat was roasted over a fire or boiled in skin or birch bark vessels, which were placed near the fire with hot rocks added to boil the water. Much of the meat was also cut into strips, and dried and stored for the winter.

The Shuswaps fished in the mountain streams, snared rabbits, and gathered rose hips, saskatoons, gooseberries, chokecherries, and other berries and roots for food. Often the berries were mashed and dried in cakes, or sun-dried and stored in skin bags for winter use. In some instances, food was wrapped in birch bark and buried in the ground near their wintering grounds, to be retrieved when winter set in. As a people who seldom used horses or canoes, the Shuswaps carried everything they owned on their backs. When they met fur traders or gold prospectors in the Tête Jaune Pass area they traded such items as fresh salmon, bear meat, beaver tails, dried skunk, mountain sheep, and berry cakes.

When Doctor Cheadle met the Shuswaps in midsummer, they were living in lodges covered with bark and matting. These were shaped like tepees, with a framework of lodgepole pine serving as a base. Sheets of bark from spruce, pine, or birch trees were

then more poles were leaned against the structure to keep the bark in place. If insufficient bark was available, mats made of woven grass or rushes were used instead.

In winter, the Shuswap abandoned their lodges and moved into semi-subterranean dwellings made of logs and earth. To construct them, they dug a hole one or two metres deep and about twenty-five metres in diameter. Logs were laid over the hole so they pointed toward the centre and sloped slightly upwards, creating a conical appearance. Branches were spread over the logs and the earth taken from the excavation was used to cover the entire structure, except for a hole in the centre, which was the only means of access. A notched log served as a ladder. These dwellings were warm and dry, even in the most severe winters. Remains of pit dwellings have been found in a number of locations on both the east and west sides of the Rockies.

Because the Shuswaps lived in small family groups, the head of the family was also their chief. He was chosen because of his hunting prowess and his ability to provide for his followers. He sometimes consulted with other family groups when going to hunt or trade, and relied upon a shaman to meet his family's religious needs. Many rituals were important

to the success of the tribe. For example, the marmot dance was performed to maintain good relations with the marmot spirit. During the dance, one man portrayed a hunter and another, the marmot, which in the end was trapped by the hunter. To guard against famine, always a danger in the Shuswaps' Rocky Mountain territory, a shaman performed a hunger dance in which he was painted like a skeleton; other songs and dances were dedicated to the success of the salmon run, to berry picking, and to communion with the spirit world.

In accordance with their marriage customs, Shuswap women were betrothed between the ages of thirteen and twenty-three, and men between the ages of twenty-two and twenty-five. No marriages were permitted among relatives, and as the *Texqokallt* was a small band, men often had difficulty finding brides. As Doctor Cheadle mentioned: "Occasionally a Rocky Mountain Shushwap makes the long and difficult journey to Kamloops on the Thompson, to seek a wife."[21] He met one old woman who had left her home as a young bride and had never been back.

The movements of the Shuswap were governed by the seasons. In late October and early November, they went to their winter camps and repaired the winter dugouts they had abandoned the previous spring. They also dug up the supplies of dried meat and berries they had stored there over the summer, and placed them on racks or in caches. They continued to hunt, concentrating on elk and other large animals. Late November marked the onset of winter, when cold weather prevented the Shuswaps from travelling great distances. That was when they hunted deer near their camps and fished through the ice of the lakes and streams; children helped by snaring rabbits and other small game. Meanwhile, women concentrated on cooking, sewing, and making clothing. Long hours were also spent telling stories and passing the history and culture of the tribe along to the children.

The weather usually improved in late February and early March, and, as the snow melted, people began leaving their winter homes. In April, families moved into their own small camps and travelled throughout their hunting grounds, collecting birch bark for new baskets and digging for edible roots. They started trapping fish as soon as the ice melted from the lakes and rivers; this was followed by trading with nearby tribes, berry picking, and salmon fishing in July and August. During this time they also continued to hunt large and small animals whenever the opportunity arose. In the autumn, everyone prepared for winter: food was dried and stored, late-ripening berries were picked, and marmots were snared for their meat for food and furs for making robes and clothing. At the end of the season, the Shuswap returned to their winter quarters and their cycle of activity was ready to begin again.

To maintain their lifestyle, the Shuswap were adept at making bows of birch or juniper wood, and arrows of saskatoon or rosewood. Arrowheads were made of chipped or flaked stone, but were replaced with metal points as soon as the fur traders arrived. Each village marked its arrows with a unique paint design applied to the shaft. Drinking vessels and baskets were made of birch bark or wood, while spoons were fashioned from mountain goat horns. Bags were made from mountain goat or bear skin, or from the paunches of deer or caribou.

By the 1890s, the Shuswap had disappeared from Jasper National Park, which was by then dominated by Iroquois/Métis hunters. At the time, Edmonton newspapers were making frequent references to the Iroquois, confirming their arrival. They described one man as being "a member of the band of Iroquois half breeds at Jasper House,"[22] pointed out that "bears are so plentiful that the Rocky Mountain Iroquois snare them without trouble," and wrote that a local guide was from "the Jasper House band of Iroquois half-breeds."[23]

The first Iroquois hunters had come from the East in the 1790s to trap for the trading companies. Once their contracts were over, some decided to stay and married local Cree and Métis women. One group settled in the upper Smoky Lake region, just east of Jasper Park, and maintained friendly relations with the local Shuswaps. After the last Shuswaps died off, the Iroquois expanded their range into the mountain area and remained there until 1910, when Jasper National Park was created and all squatters were evicted. These Iroquois families then moved to the Grande Cache area where many of their descendants remain today.

On the British Columbia side of the Rockies, when the local Shuswaps died out, others moved into the region from the west. In the 1850s, Paul Ignatius Kinbasket brought a band of Shuswaps into the Windermere district from Adams Lake, northeast of Kamloops. They lived for a time at Kinbasket Lake, then moved south to Windermere, where they became allies of the local Kootenay bands. In 1887, the local Indian agent reported, "A small offshoot from the Shuswap Indians reside in this district; they live upon a reserve at Columbia lakes at the north portion of the grass country. Nothing but good can be said of these Shuswaps, who are known as the Kinbasket's Band. They pay great attention to their farms and are very industrious … The men earn money during the summer as packers; and all trap and hunt during a portion of the winter."[24]

Today, these Rocky Mountain Shuswaps live on a reserve near Lake Windermere and have a population of between two hundred and three hundred people. There they dwell comfortably in modern frame houses and mobile homes.

THE LOST TRIBE

The Jasper National Park area was once occupied by a band of Shuswap Indians known as the Snares. They were a quiet, inoffensive people who, by the mid-nineteenth century, had been virtually destroyed by their enemies.

They were a branch of the much larger Shuswap nation and in the late 1700s they ranged on both sides of the Rockies near Yellowhead Pass and south to Lake Windermere. However, the hostility of their enemies forced them to flee and in 1811, fur trader Alexander Henry noted that they had "retired northward to an uninhabited part of the Rocky mountains, where they continue to wander, a most wretched and defenseless people, who never war upon any of their neighbours."[25]

According to one observer, they lived in winter pit dwellings and made snares of green hides to trap bighorn sheep, moose, and deer. Even when other tribes were armed with muzzle-loading guns, the Snares still used bows and arrows. During this time they hunted and fished in what is now Jasper National Park, where they were a particular target of the Crees and Stoneys. For example, in 1811, Alexander Henry met a group of Crees setting out to attack the Snares. "These are defenseless Indians, who know not the use of firearms," he wrote, "have only bows and arrows, and are scattered in small camps of three and four tents—an easy prey to the Crees. But their country is so nearly destitute of animals that the Crees suffer from famine when they go to war upon these people and are frequently obliged to return before they can fall upon them."[26]

About 1840, most of the Snares—consisting of about twenty families—were hunting in and around the present Jasper town site while some Stoneys were camped beside Lake Brule, twenty kilometres northeast. During the autumn, the Stoneys sent a message to the Snares proposing that a peace treaty be made between the two tribes. They suggested that a feast be held near the mouth of what is now called Snake Indian River. (This river should probably be called the Snare Indian River, as "Snake" refers to Shoshoni Indians who live far to the south, in Idaho.) Both parties were to come to the treaty grounds unarmed.

According to fur trader Walter Moberly, the Stoneys concealed their guns under their blankets and at a prearranged signal opened fire on their hapless neighbours. They then rushed to the Snare camp where they wiped out anyone who had not already fled into the bush. Three young women were captured, tied up, and placed in a tent, to be killed at a scalp dance the next day.[27] During the night, they escaped and travelled downstream as far as the junction of the Athabasca and Berland rivers. There they parted ways, with two building a raft to float down the Athabasca; they were never heard from again. The third, armed only with a knife, travelled up the Berland for about twenty-five kilometres and there she made a winter camp. She gathered berries, killed a few squirrels, made snares from their tails, and used them for catching rabbits. She killed porcupines and dried their flesh, and made a robe from woven rabbit skins. She survived the long cold winter by herself and the following spring she crossed the Rockies to join a friendly Shuswap camp at Tête Jaune Cache. It was there that fur trader Moberly met her about 1859, encamped with a small band of Shuswaps.[28]

Eleven men, women, and children managed to escape the initial attack of the Stoneys, among them their chief *Assannitchay*, or Capote Blanc. When artist Paul Kane met him in 1846, he painted his portrait and described him as "a very simple, kind-hearted old man, with whom I became very friendly."[29] After the massacre, he took refuge at the Hudson's Bay post at Jasper House and was periodically employed by the traders to guide parties through the mountains. He was also a proficient hunter. Kane met him again a year later when Capote Blanc and two Shuswaps were hunting near Boat Encampment, north of the present town of Golden. "Capote Blanc had been very successful in his hunt," wrote Kane, "and had a large stock of dried moose meat and beavers' tails, with which he supplied us abundantly."[30]

In 1859, James Hector, explorer for the Palliser Expedition, was travelling along the Columbia River near the site of present-day Golden when he met Capote Blanc. He wrote:

> After we encamped we heard some one calling out down by the river, and found that a couple of Shouswap Indians had heard us firing and had come up the river in a rough "dug out" wooden canoe, in search of us. We were very fortunate, as it proved to be Capôt Blanc, the chief, who was for a long time the Jasper House guide for crossing the mountains. The other Indian was his son … They staid with us all night, and in exchange for some tobacco and ammunition gave us some of the flesh of a black bear they had just killed … We also got some dried sifleurs [marmot] and goat's flesh …[31]

Capote Blanc, his son, and the escaped woman were the last survivors of the Snare band. When they died, the band disappeared forever. The lands near Jasper, which became vacant after the massacre, were eventually taken over by Métis and Iroquois hunters.

On 5 November 1846, when artist Paul
Kane was at Jasper House, he wrote in his
diary: "The Indians about here do not number above fifteen or twenty; they are the
Shoo-Schawp tribe, and their chief, of
whom I made a sketch, is called 'Capote
Blanc' by the voyageurs—in their own language it is Assannitchay, but means the
same." Capote Blanc was one of the last
survivors of the Snare band that hunted in
the present Jasper National Park.

—Peabody Museum, Harvard University, 41-72-
10/392.

In the 1890s, these six chiefs from the British Columbia interior were photographed after they had met with government officials. Pierre Kinbasket, of the Shuswap Reserve, is in the front row, extreme right. Others in the front row, left to right, are Abel Morning Star, a Kootenay from Columbia Lake, and Chief Francois, a Kootenay from St. Mary's Reserve. In the back row, left to right, are Thunderbird, from Cranbrook, and Three Feathers and Alexander, from Creston.

—*Windermere District Historical Society, C338.*

Twin brothers Charles, left, and Pierre Kinbasket were leaders of the two main families on the Shuswap Reserve at the turn of the century. Charles holds a small stone pipe while his brother Pierre holds the larger council pipe. Both men were elected chiefs of the band in 1889. According to Pierre's granddaughter, "Hundreds of Indians attended the council and the Chief and his advisors sat around the council rug. The meeting opened in silence while the peace pipe, filled with kinikinick, was passed from mouth to mouth among those entitled to its use. Each Indian took three or four puffs. At last the issue to be decided was broached."

—*Glenbow Archives, NA-2908-1.*

Shuswap and Kootenay Indians gather for a celebration in the 1920s. Their costumes include Plains Indian headdresses, beaded ties and collars, beaded vests, and elk tooth dresses. The boy at left wears an outfit which is a mixture of cowboy and Indian.

—*Glenbow Archives, NA-1135-47.*

A Shuswap woman, Maria Eugene, at left, joins with Margaret Jimmy from the Kootenay tribe to take part in ceremonies at Lake Windermere in 1922. Both women have heavily beaded dresses, but only the Kootenay horse is decorated. Notice the bells on the horse's hooves.

—*Glenbow Archives, NA-1135-12.*

This Ktunaxa-Kinbasket camp was photographed near the Elk River, about 1898.

—*Fort Steele Historic Park Archives, FS.5.12.*

The Shuswaps were early converts to Christianity and life on their reserve centred around the mission. Here, Charles Kinbasket, or Tuelna, holds a crucifix as he sits outside the church with his wife Suzette.

—*Windermere District Historical Society, C336.*

Members of the Shuswap band are seen here at a church picnic at the turn of the century. Left to right are Marianne Kinbasket, her grandchildren Catherine and Rosie Palmer, her daughter Amelia Palmer, Father Evans, and Rosalee Kinbasket.

—Windermere District Historical Society, C337.

The Catholic church on the Shuswap Reserve, just north of Invermere, BC, is a reminder of the early conversion of this band to Christianity, and their close affiliation with the church over the years. This view was taken in 1998.

—H. Dempsey Collection.

The Shuswaps, Kootenays, and Stoneys of the Rocky Mountains often made tepees covered with tree bark or reed matting. At right is a typical tepee where sheets of spruce bark have been applied in overlapping strips and more poles laid against the structure to keep the bark in place. This was exhibited by Stoneys at the Banff Indian Days in 1938. Below is a lodge made of matting used by a Kootenay family. Both types also were common to the Shuswaps.

—Glenbow Archives, NA-7-55 and NA-1141-4.

Marianne Kinbasket, a Shuswap from the Kamloops area, moved to the Windermere valley when she married the chief of the tribe. She was described as a strong woman, physically and mentally, who was a staunch Catholic but still believed in the traditional religion of her people. She planted her garden according to the phases of the moon and considered all growing things to be sacred. She believed that those who performed evil deeds were reincarnated as spiders.

—*Windermere District Historical Society, A96.*

Chief Pierre Kinbasket and his wife Marianne are seen in front of their log cabin on the Shuswap Reserve, about 1910. Seated beside them in a chair is the Indian agent. As it is summer time, the family has pitched their tepee in the yard and are cooking outside.

—Glenbow Archives, NA-2908-2.

Amelia and Angelique Kinbasket, seen here at the turn of the century, were daughters of the Shuswap chief at Invermere. Amelia later married William Palmer, a settler in the Windermere valley.

—Windermere District Historical Society, C176.

As a young woman, Rose Kinbasket was denied the chance to marry her sweetheart, so she remained single until she was killed in a horse race in Vancouver. At that time, the family believed the Kinbaskets had been cursed by a Stoney when Rose's uncle refused to sell him a palomino horse. After the argument, the palomino died and a number of the family were killed in horse-related accidents.

—*Windermere District Historical Society, C178.*

Maras Kinbasket was a member of the leading family on the Shuswap Reserve. In 1898, the Indian agent reported that "the members of this small band still keep the lead for industry and progress. They depend upon cattle, horses and farming as their means of living. They have the best kept farms in the agency, and their land is easily cultivated and is well supplied with water for irrigation, and their crops seldom fail."

—*Windermere District Historical Society, C177.*

The Saukuitapix, or Blackfoot Nation

The Blackfoot nation is made up of three tribes that, for generations, dominated the western plains. These are the *Siksikau* or Blackfoot proper; the *Kainaiwa* or Bloods; and the *Pikuni* or Peigans. Together they occupied a vast hunting ground, which extended from the Red Deer River in the north to the Missouri River in the south, and from the Cypress Hills in the east to the Rocky Mountains in the west. The Blackfoot proper usually hunted in the northeast section of their territory and ventured into the mountains only when carrying out raids against the Stoney Indians or when searching for lodgepole pine for tepee poles. The Peigans hunted along the foothills and mountains south into Montana, while the Bloods ranged from what is now Waterton National Park, east to what is now Medicine Hat. These two Blackfoot tribes were most familiar with the Rockies and its passes that led to the lands of their enemies, the Kootenays. In Blackfoot mythology, the Rockies were created by the trickster *Napi* and were known as the "Backbone of the World."

The life of the Blackfoot revolved around the buffalo, which provided meat for food, skins for lodges and clothing, bones for handles and utensils, and rawhide for bags. Before the Blackfoot acquired horses in the early 1700s, they hunted by stalking or impoundment. When stalking, a hunter covered himself with a buffalo calf skin and approached the herd, making noises like a calf in distress. Curious cows came forward to see whose calf was suffering, and before they realized the danger, one or more of them was killed with well-placed arrows.

The impoundment of buffalo was a communal activity. To succeed, the Blackfoot always chose a steep embankment, often along the foothills, and built a corral at the bottom. Then two men were sent out to drive the herd and as the animals approached the site, other hunters hiding behind rock piles jumped up and stampeded them over the cliff. Those not killed by the fall were dispatched by hunters waiting below. The animals were then butchered and their meat prepared for preservation. Sometimes it was simply cut into long, thin strips and dried. Other times it was dried, pulverized, and mixed with crushed, dried berries and hot fat. This dish, called pemmican, was stored in rawhide bags for use during the winter. It could be eaten dry or mixed with water to produce a soup called *rugaboo*.

After the Blackfoot obtained horses for transportation, the chase became their favourite method of hunting. A man astride a well-trained horse, called a buffalo runner, dashed into a herd of fleeing buffalo and picked out a fat cow. He rode up beside it, guiding the horse only with his knees, often getting so close that his leg brushed against the animal's side. He then shot an arrow into its heart and veered his horse away so it would not be struck by the falling beast. Without pausing, he galloped ahead to catch other animals, killing as many as three or four in a single run. Each hunter had his own method of marking his arrows, so after the chase he could identify his kills and set to work with his wife to do the butchering.

A Peigan Indian named *Kainaikwan* described an average year in the life of a Blackfoot camp in the

1860s. In the spring, when the grass was green and their horses had regained the weight they had lost over the winter, the Peigans left the foothills and set out for the open prairies to hunt buffalo. After a kill, the kidneys and backfat were eaten first, as delicacies. Then, as the Blackfoot followed the herds, they dried and stored the extra meat. Meanwhile, women who needed new tepees began to collect hides and tan them. In the summer, when the berries were ripe, they went to the coulees to pick saskatoons, chokecherries, and white berries. One of their favourite dishes was made by breaking open leg bones, boiling the marrow fat, and mixing it with chokecherries.

When the women had enough hides for their new tepees, the band moved westward toward the mountains to cut poles. One of their most popular places was located beside what is now Waterton National Park, at a ridge they called Pole Haven. Once the poles had been cut, the newly-made tepees were stretched over the frames and smoky fires lit inside until the skins were cured. Then, according to *Kainaikwan*:

> They moved closer to the mountains just as the leaves were beginning to turn in colour. Here they hunted black tailed deer, elk, and moose. When the first snows came, they began to hurry, moving down to the lower country to camp along the river. There they watched to see where the buffalo were going to spend the winter and they settled near them.[32]

Before the snows arrived, the women busily engaged in tanning hides to make clothing and robes. With the first frost, they harvested bullberries by placing robes under the bushes and beating the branches until the berries fell off. Meanwhile, children peeled the bark from trees and ate the inner bark as a candy. They also dug for roots, which they ate, and black alkali soil, which they sucked as a treat.

During the winter, the main activities of the women consisted of collecting firewood and fetching water. Meanwhile, the men tended the horse herds and hunted buffalo whenever the weather permitted. They also hunted elk, antelope, and deer, but they preferred buffalo. Then, with the arrival of spring, the whole cycle of activity was repeated.

Because they controlled such vast hunting grounds, the Blackfoot were frequently at war, protecting them: Crees and Metis attacked from the north, Kootenays and Stoneys from the west, Crows and Shoshoni from the south, and Assiniboine and Sioux from the east. In addition, young Blackfoot warriors were constantly raiding other tribes for horses, adding to the level of conflict. Consequently, a boy learned about war from the time he could walk. In the winter, elders told stories that extolled the exploits of great warriors and the virtues of defeating enemies in battle. Not surprisingly, boys' games usually had a warlike base: two teams having a mud fight, "raiding" meat drying on a rack, or playing spin top, where each top represented a warrior in battle. Then, when they were about thirteen years old, boys were encouraged to join a horse-raiding party as a servant. They did not take part in the actual attack, but carried water, made fires, and repaired moccasins for the older warriors while they were on the trail. After one or two such journeys, a young man was finally permitted to take an active part in raiding expeditions.

Even though it may have been easier to raid enemy camps on the open plains, the Bloods and Peigans often crossed the mountains to attack the Kootenays because of the fine quality of their horses. To do so, the plainsmen risked discovery while travelling through the mountain passes and faced the danger of starvation if game could not be found along the trail.

In the 1860s, a Peigan named Mad Wolf led a war party on a raid across the mountains and they were on their way home with captured horses when they suddenly heard the sounds of horsemen. The Peigans immediately hid beside the trail and writer Walter McClintock explained what happened next. "A war party of Kutenai were returning from an expedition into the Blackfeet country," he said. "They ran into the ambush and there was a fierce battle. Mad Wolf, as chief of the expedition, was entitled to the first shot. He singled out the leader, but the Kutenai chief was very brave. Although badly wounded, he ran into the thick woods where Mad Wolf killed him."[33]

The Peigans were pressed hard by the Kootenays, but under Mad Wolf's leadership, they killed the entire party, except for one old woman. They painted her face black, gave her food and clothing, and set her free as their gift to the Sun spirit for giving them a victory.

In another instance, the lack of knowledge of the mountain country was disastrous to a Blackfoot war party of eight young men. They raided a Kootenay camp and hurried back through the main pass in the mountains, not realizing that the trail took a wide curve and that there was a shortcut over the mountain. However, their Kootenay pursuers knew about the shortcut, and arrived at the fork in the trail before the Blackfoot. As their enemies approached, the Kootenays opened fire and killed seven of them on the spot. The eighth was lagging behind, and when he heard the gunfire he hid in the trees and escaped. He had stolen the best racehorse in the Kootenay camp and its owner was unwilling to give it up, so the wronged Kootenay went after the remaining Blackfoot by himself. He discovered the hoofprints of his horse in the early morning frost and again he knew a shortcut that would put him

ahead of the Blackfoot. They met in a narrow canyon, the Kootenay riding in from the east. The Blackfoot shot first and missed, but the Kootenay didn't miss with his shot. He killed his enemy, scalped him, and rode back in triumph on his favourite horse.[34]

On yet another occasion, a war party of Peigans saw some Kootenays hunting buffalo on the east side of the Rockies. When the Kootenays realized they had been discovered by their enemy, they headed for the closest mountain pass, although their medicine man warned them to take a different route. Their chief, Rose Hips, or Baptiste, refused, and led his followers to the fork of a river where, unknown to him, the Peigans lay in ambush. They opened fire, killed the chief, and succeeded in capturing an old woman. When she told them the name of the dead chief they were so elated that they had slain someone so important, they gave her the chief's blanket and sent her back to her people to inform them of his death.[35]

As far as their lifestyle was concerned, the Blackfoot were luckier than other Alberta tribes. Their hunting grounds were home to very few fur-bearing animals, so fur traders tended to ignore them and did not try to change their way of life, as they did with the woodland and mountain tribes. The first trading posts were established on the North Saskatchewan River, at Fort Edmonton, in 1795, and at Rocky Mountain House four years later. Both were well beyond Blackfoot hunting grounds. Twice a year, the Blackfoot took dried meat, buffalo robes, and horses to trade for knives, axes, guns, and other trade goods.

In 1831, the Americans built a post on the Missouri River to trade with the Blackfoot and for the next forty years, the tribes had the choice of dealing with the British to the north, or with the Americans to the south. They quickly became astute traders, obtaining Sheffield steel knives and woollen blankets from the Hudson's Bay Company, and ammunition, gun powder, and cotton goods from the Americans. To compete, the British built Peagan Post in 1832, just east of what now is Banff National Park, but the Blackfoot did not want white men living within their territory and it closed a short time later.

Major changes in the Blackfoot way of life occurred in the 1860s when the Americans found gold in Montana. The land was flooded with prospectors and the inevitable clashes occurred. Any miners travelling along the edge of the Rockies risked being killed. In fact, several Americans were slain while prospecting near what today is Waterton National Park, while a whole party was wiped out north of Pincher Creek at a site now known as Massacre Butte. In 1869, misery came to the Blackfoot when they were invaded by free traders whose main stock-in-trade was cheap whiskey. Forts with such colourful names as Whoop-Up, Slide Out, and Standoff were built in the Lethbridge area and the traders created such havoc that, in 1874, the North-West Mounted Police were sent west to restore law and order.

In 1877, the tribes of the Blackfoot nation, as well as the Stoneys and Sarcees (or *Tsuu T'ina*), came together at Blackfoot Crossing to sign Treaty No. Seven with the federal government. Then, with the disappearance of the last buffalo herds three years later, the tribes were obliged to settle on reserves. The Blackfoot proper located east of Calgary, the Peigans near the mouth of the Crowsnest Pass, and the Bloods southwest of Lethbridge. In addition, the Bloods and Blackfoot obtained timber lands within the boundaries of what now are Waterton and Banff National Parks, and the Peigans in the Porcupine Hills.

Over the years, the Blackfoot tribes turned to ranching and farming. Because of their large reserves—the Blood Reserve is the largest in Canada—the Blackfoot have been able to retain much of their traditional culture. They still hold the Sun Dance, wear white buckskin costumes to pow-wows and Indian Days, speak their own language as well as English, and display their love of horses through rodeos and races.

LEGEND OF SLEEPING INDIAN MOUNTAIN

Mount Richards, on the west side of Waterton Lakes in Waterton National Park, was originally known as Sleeping Indian Mountain because of the profile of an Indian head visible on its eastern ridge.

According to legend, back in the "dog days" before Indians had horses, a marriage had been arranged between *Piksiaki* or Bird Woman, daughter of a Blackfoot Indian chief, and *Apaiitsikin* or Weasel Moccasin, son of a prominent Blood leader. The wedding was seen as an important union that would cement relations between the two tribes. However, Bird Woman was in love with a poor young man named *Awaksiomukan*, or Running Antelope.

Bird Woman went to her father and begged for permission to marry the poor young man, but he coldly refused. He wanted the Bloods to be his allies and was not concerned about his daughter's personal desires.

On the appointed day, Weasel Moccasin and his family arrived at the Blackfoot camp with gifts of robes, furs, clothing, spears, and shields. During the celebrations and feasting, Bird Woman slipped away to meet her lover and to tell him of her father's decision. Not to be dissuaded, Running Antelope convinced the woman to elope with him, to run away while everybody was celebrating. They would cross the mountains—the backbone of the world—and live among the people who inhabited the warmer lands to the west.

The two set out for the mountains, but they had not gone far when Bird Woman was missed. Guessing what had happened, her angry father called the Blackfoot and Blood warriors to go in pursuit of the fleeing couple, and to slay Running Antelope. At that time, they were camped on the open prairie, where they could see great distances. Soon the warriors could discern two tiny dots in the distance and hurried to catch the pair before they got to the Rockies. When Running Antelope saw they were being pursued, he prayed to the Sun spirit and offered himself as a sacrifice if their lives were spared. In response, a huge thunderstorm burst out from the mountains and a deluge of water poured down on the prairies, until a huge lake stood between the warriors and the two lovers.

Not to be thwarted, the Bloods and Blackfoot made rafts from cottonwood trees that lined the lake and soon they were again on the trail of the fleeing couple. By this time Bird Woman and Running Antelope had almost reached the mountains, but the young man knew their enemies would capture them before they could find safety in the rugged canyons. Again he turned to the Sun spirit for help but this time he was told that the only way to save the girl was to let her join the Star People. In order to do this, Running Antelope had to stay behind to prevent the Bloods and Blackfoot from pursuing her. When he agreed, the young man found himself growing larger and larger until he became a huge mountain which blocked the pathway of their pursuers. Meanwhile, Bird Woman climbed high into the mountains until she reached the clouds. There she joined the Star People and became one of the many stars of the night sky. As for her lover, Running Antelope, his face appears on the side of Sleeping Indian Mountain, where he constantly remains on guard to protect his beloved Bird Woman.[36]

This view of a Blood Sun Dance in the 1880s was taken by ex-Mounted Policeman George Anderton. At right is the framework of the Sun Dance lodge being readied for sacred ceremonies. Note that the travois, usually drawn by horses, have been placed as tripods to make sun shades.

—*Provincial Archives of Alberta, A18697.*

Spotted Eagle with his two wives, Black Horn Woman and Longtime Gun Woman, in 1892. Spotted Eagle gave gifts of seven horses when he married each of them. Note that his hair is braided into a fore-top, which was worn during wartime to challenge enemies to try to take his scalp.

—*Glenbow Archives, NA-668-21.*

This family of Blackfoot women and children was camped on the open prairies, about 1881, likely while the men were away hunting.

—*United Church of Canada Archives, 93.049 P/957.*

Crooked Rib, a Blood Indian, seen here in the 1880s, wears an American peace treaty medal given when the Blackfoot nation made a treaty in 1855. Like most Plains Indians, he prized his repeating rifle and belt of cartridges.

—*H. Dempsey Collection.*

Bear Shield, or Kyi-aotan, a Blood Indian, is seen with a shirt which could be worn only by members of the Braves Warrior Society. Around his neck hangs a bone whistle, indicating his leadership in the society, while the square beaded pouch at his chest contains a mirror used for signalling.

—*H. Dempsey Collection.*

Bull Back, Chief of Blood Indians, North-west Territory, British Possessions.

This rare view shows an encampment of Blood Indians at Fort Whoop-Up in the 1870s. The bastion of the whiskey fort can be seen in the background. The lodge, known as the Many Striped Tepee, was owned by Bull Back Fat, leader of the All Short People band. He and his extended family are in the group. At this time, the Bloods were still a nomadic people, so the presence of a baby carriage was highly unusual.

—*Hook View Company, 511.*

**This is a typical Blackfoot encampment, photographed in
1885. It was obviously a hot day, for the owners of the
tepee in the foreground at right have fashioned two dog
travois to make a sun shade. At left, two horse travois
are kept off the ground so they will not rot.**

—*Glenbow Archives, NA-4967-58.*

Young Pine was one of the leading men of the Blood tribe. In this view, taken in the 1890s, he carries a ceremonial spear indicating his membership in the Braves Warrior Society and wears a shirt decorated with human hair.

—United Church of Canada Archives, 93.049 P/911.

The most sacred ceremonies of the Blackfoot nation took place at the annual Sun Dance, at which time the various religious societies performed their rites. Methodist missionary John Maclean obtained this photograph of the women's society lodge in the 1890s. It is made of tepee canvas with horse travois forming the basic framework. The ceremonies inside the lodge were secret, viewed only by members of the women's society and their helpers.

—United Church of Canada Archives, 93.049 P/965.

Eagle Arrow was a warrior who later became a scout for the North-West Mounted Police. When photographed by T.J. Hileman in 1924, he was showing signs of blindness, caused by glaucoma, a common disease in the tribe.

—Glenbow Archives, NB-21-4.

After the Bloods settled on their reserve in the early 1880s, many were encouraged to give up their firearms. Big Calf, seen here in the 1890s, was one of those who refused, and by 1896 he still prized his rim-fire repeating rifle. The amulet he wears in his hair is made of leather, weasel skins, and feathers.

—*United Church of Canada Archives, 93.049 P/918.*

James Willard Schultz, who had married a Piegan woman in the 1880s, wrote more than three dozen novels about Blackfoot Indian life. He is seen here at Waterton Park with members of the Blood tribe. Left to right are Bobtail Chief and his wife, Mrs. Weasel Tail, Schultz, Many Mules, and Weasel Tail.

—H. Dempsey Collection.

By the 1890s, many Blackfoot Indians lived in log houses instead of tepees. Here, Wolf Child, his wife, and daughter, members of the Blood tribe, pose in front of their cabin. Because this photo was taken by a Catholic missionary, the frame which Wolf Child holds may be a religious picture.

—*Provincial Archives of Alberta, OB.6552.*

**Blood Indians sit for photographer W.E. Hook
in the 1870s in front of Fort Whoop-Up, a
notorious whiskey-trading post located near
the site of present-day Lethbridge.**

—*Hook View Company, 506.*

This Blackfoot Indian, photographed about 1887 by Alex Ross, bears all the symbols of his warrior society. He wears skunk skin garters, carries a ceremonial sword, and has a beaded shirt which has a light side to symbolize day and a dark side for night.

—*Glenbow Archives, NA-1906-1.*

Black Plume, or Siksapohp, was a leading member of the Blood tribe. In this formal studio picture taken in the 1890s, he wears his own leggings and moccasins, but is clad in a smoked buckskin jacket that was a prop of photographer Fred Steele. Photos exist of a number of prominent leaders wearing the same jacket.

—*United Church of Canada Archives, 93.049 P/956.*

Entitled "Blood Indian Warrior," this is a
studio picture of Flying Chief, a Blood
Indian whose parents were killed in an
Indian raid and who was adopted by white
traders. He was given the name of Joe
Healy and was one of the first educated
members of his tribe.

—*United Church of Canada Archives, 93.049 P/955.*

Children from the Blood Reserve gather in front of the Catholic mission at Standoff in the 1890s.

—Provincial Archives of Alberta, OB.8835.

Methodist John Maclean entitled this photo "Three of My School Lads." They attended his mission school on the Blood Reserve in the 1880s. Note that the horse at left is controlled by a "war bridle," a braided rawhide lariat with two half hitches placed in the horse's mouth and tightened around the lower jaw.

—United Church of Canada Archives, 93.049 P/948.

Students from the Blood Indian mission school attended summer camps at Waterton National Park. Here, six girls walk along a mountain pathway in 1936. Left to right: Irene Prairie Chicken, Irene White Calf, Miss Buckskin, Nora Gladstone, Winnie Cole, and Ada Wings.

—P. Dempsey Collection.

Blood Indian students and staff gather at a Waterton Lakes signpost in the 1920s. Left to right, front row are: Gladys Brave Rock and Gertie Weir; second row, Miss Cathcart (teacher), Mabel Mistaken Chief, Annie Wolf Plume, and unknown; third row, Grace Tallow and a teacher; and back row, Iva Spear Chief and unknown. The Bloods have timber lands within the park and held summer camps there.

—P. Dempsey Collection.

Red Crow was the great chief of the Blood tribe from 1870 until his death in 1900. In this photograph, he wears a scarlet uniform provided by the Indian Department, a large medal given to him at the signing of the Blackfoot treaty in 1877, and other medals presented by prominent visitors to his reserve. Red Crow was proud of the fact that he had been in thirty-seven battles and was never wounded.

—*Glenbow Archives, NA-56-1.*

Bull Plume, or Stomaksisaohp, was a leading chief of the Peigan tribe. He was a ceremonialist and keeper of the Blackfoot winter counts (a method of recording dates). In this photograph he wears a shirt decorated with wild turnips of the type used in the Sun Dance ceremonies. Both his shirt and leggings are trimmed with weasel skins while around his neck he wears a choker made of buffalo teeth.

—*Glenbow Archives, NB-11-3.*

Shot Both Sides was head chief of the Blood tribe from 1913 to 1956. As a young man, he took part in five raids against his enemies. In one of these raids, he and two companions captured some horses from a Gros Ventre camp and travelled non-stop for two days to return to their own hunting grounds. This photograph was taken by T.J. Hileman in 1927.

—*Glenbow Archives, NB-21-13.*

Three women and a child from the Blackfoot tribe wear clothing typical of their people. Photographed in Calgary in 1912, the woman at left has a dress made of Hudson's Bay Company wool stroud cloth, while the others wear dresses of cotton. The dress of the woman at the right has a yoke which is completely covered with beads and is decorated with thimbles. Notice that the women wear their hair parted in the middle and hanging in front. Men preferred a pompadour style.

—*Glenbow Archives, NA-768-4.*

Lacking refrigeration, the Blackfoot method of preserving meat was by sun drying. Here, the meat is high on a rack where it is out of the reach of dogs. Once dried, it could be made into pemmican or stored for later use. This view was taken on the Blood Reserve in the 1920s.

—*Glenbow Archives, NA-879-5.*

In the 1920s, this Blood woman decided to join parades and festivals to recreate an image of the past. Heavy Face, wife of White Calf, wears a canvas dress and a robe of worn out buffalo hide while she prepares her dog travois for a parade.

—*H. Dempsey Collection.*

One Gun was a respected elder of the Blackfoot tribe, seen here in the 1920s. His father, Good Old Man, was wealthy and bestowed religious gifts on him. When he was twelve, One Gun received a weasel tail suit and as soon as he became a teenager, his father gave twenty-seven horses for a medicine pipe and sixteen horses for a horned headdress. When he was fifteen, his father gave him his most sacred possession, a tiny ammonite, or buffalo stone, which had protected him from harm throughout his years as a warrior. One Gun kept this object for the rest of his own life. Born too late to be a warrior, he became a successful farmer and was an active participant in the annual Sun Dance.

—*H. Dempsey Collection.*

Distant Voice, or Piyiskini, a member of the Blackfoot tribe, is seen here in the 1920s. As a young man, he was in a war party which attacked some Cree hunters. They trapped their enemies beside a small lake where the Crees dug trenches, and in hand-to-hand combat, Distant Voice shot and wounded one of the Crees with a bow and arrow. When it was over, one Cree had been killed but none of the Blackfoot war party was injured.

—H. Dempsey Collection.

To permit tourists to enjoy the colour and pageantry of the Blackfoot nation, the Prince of Wales Hotel in Waterton National Park invited Indians to perform dances and ceremonies. Here, a group from the Peigan Reserve put on a show in the 1930s, amid the pictographs and other Indian decor of the hotel.

—H. Dempsey Collection.

Blood Indians greet New York artist Winold Reiss at Waterton Lakes in 1935. Left to right are: Owns Different Horses, Riding Black Horses, Falling Over a Bank, unknown man and child, Tjark Reiss, Winold Reiss, unknown, Takes a Good Run (Mrs. Riding Black Horses), Head Chief Shot Both Sides, unknown, Plume, Jack Low Horn, and Gros Ventre Boy.

—H. Dempsey Collection.

In the 1940s, many Peigan Indians lived in log cabins such as this one. Solidly built of spruce logs brought from the mountains, such cabins provided protection against the bitter winter weather.

—*H. Dempsey Collection.*

The Blackfoot had a great affinity for Chief Mountain, which was considered to be the home of the thunder spirit. Here Jim Black Plume, a member of the Blood tribe, is seen on the slopes of the mountain in 1953.

—*H. Dempsey Collection.*

Notes

1. *Annual Report of the Department of Indian Affairs for the Year ended March 31, 1912* (Ottawa: King's Printer, 1912), 175, 191, 219–21.

2. Elizabeth Parker, "The Canadian Alps," *Calgary Herald*, 25 July 1901.

3. Marius Barbeau, *Indian Days on the Western Prairies* (Ottawa: National Museum of Canada, 1960), 143.

4. *Ibid.*, 1960, 111–12.

5. John Laurie, "The Stony Indians of Alberta." Manuscript in John Laurie Papers, Glenbow Archives.

6. Earl of Southesk, *Saskatchewan and the Rocky Mountains* (Edinburgh: Edmonston and Douglas, 1875), 245.

7. *Calgary Herald*, 19 June 1895.

8. *Ibid.*

9. Jon Whyte, *Indians in the Rockies* (Banff: Altitude Publishing Ltd., 1985), 72.

10. *Calgary Herald*, 17 July 1922.

11. Ella Elizabeth Clark, *Indian Legends of Canada* (Toronto: McClelland & Stewart, 1960), 96.

12. *Ibid.*, 97.

13. Eliott Coues, ed., *New Light on the Early History of the Greater Northwest: The Manuscript Journals of Alexander Henry, Fur Trader of the Northwest Company, and of David Thompson, Official Geographer and Explorer of the same Company, 1799–1814* (New York: Francis P. Harper, 1897), 703.

14. "Journal of a Journey over Land from Buckingham House to the Rocky Mountains in 1792 & 3," by Peter Fidler. Hudson's Bay Company Archives, Provincial Archives of Manitoba. Entry for 31 December 1792.

15. Irene M. Spry, ed., *The Papers of The Palliser Expedition, 1857–1860* (Toronto: The Champlain Society, 1968), 462–63.

16. W. Langdon Kihn, "Kootenay Legend of the Valley of the Twin Lakes (Akiskanook)," *Indian Days on the Western Prairies*, ed. Marius Barbeau (Ottawa: National Museum of Canada, 1960), 183–88.

17. Viscount Milton and W.B. Cheadle, *The North-West Passage by Land* (London: Cassell, Petter, and Galpin, 1865), 240.

18. *Ibid.*, 241.

19. *Ibid.*, 242.

20. Marie Matthew, ed., *Introduction to the Shuswap* (Kamloops: Secwepemc Cultural Education Society, 1986), 2.

21. Viscount Milton, *op.cit.*, 240.

22. *Edmonton Bulletin*, 9 October 1893.

23. *Ibid.*, 26 October 1896.

24. Report of Michael Phillipps, Kootenay Agency, 2 August 1887. *Annual Report of the Department of Indian Affairs for the Year Ended December 31, 1887.* Ottawa, 1888, p.122.

25. Elliott Coues, ed., *The Manuscript Journals of Alexander Henry, Fur Trader of the Northwest Company, and of David Thompson, Official Geographer and Explorer of the same Company, 1799–1814* (New York: Francis P. Harper, 1897), 704.

26. *Ibid.*, 1897, 596.

27. Walter Moberly, *When Fur Was King* (New York: E.P. Dutton & Co., 1929), 112.

28. *Ibid.*, 1929, 111.

29. J. Russell Harper, ed., *Paul Kane's Frontier* (Toronto: University of Toronto Press, 1971), 87.

30. *Ibid.*, 1971, 129.

31. Irene M. Spry, *The Palliser Expedition, 1847–1860* (Toronto: The Champlain Society, 1968), 455–56.

32. Paraphrased from C.C. Uhlenbeck, *A New Series of Blackfoot Texts* (Amsterdam: Johannes Müller, 1912).

33. Walter McClintock, *The Old North Trail* (London: Macmillan and Co., 1910), 52.

34. Marius Barbeau, *Indian Days on the Western Prairies* (Ottawa: National Museum of Canada, 1960), 130–31.

35. Claude Schaeffer Papers, book II, file 4, box 17, Glenbow Archives.

36. Charles Kettles, "The Legend of Indian Head," *Lethbridge Herald*, 15 September 1922.

About the Author

Hugh A. Dempsey is a well-known historian, writer, and researcher. Raised and educated in Edmonton, he became a reporter and later an editor for the daily *Edmonton Bulletin*. In 1956 he was appointed the first archivist of the Glenbow Foundation in Calgary and spent thirty-five years with that organization, retiring in 1991 as Associate Director of the Glenbow Museum. He has been editor of the quarterly *Alberta History* since 1956 and is the author of fourteen books, including *Indian Tribes of Alberta, Red Crow: Warrior Chief, The Amazing Death of Calf Shirt and Other Blackfoot Stories*, and *The Golden Age of the Canadian Cowboy*. He is an honorary chief of the Blood tribe, a recipient of the Order of Canada, and has an honorary doctorate from the University of Calgary. His wife, Pauline, is a member of the Blood tribe and a granddaughter of the great leader, Flying Chief. The Dempseys have five grown children, all living in Alberta.